The Pledge of Allegiance

For Jason, who inspired me,

and Jay, who encouraged me.

BRIGHT SKY PRESS

Box 416, Albany, Texas 76430

10   9   8   7   6   5   4   3   2   1

Library of Congress Cataloging-in-Publication Data

Clack, Barbra, 1952–
    The Pledge of Allegiance / written & illustrated by Barbra Clack.
      p. cm.
    ISBN 1-931721-48-3 (alk. paper)
1. Bellamy, Francis. Pledge of Allegiance to the Flag—Juvenile literature. 2. Emblems,
    National—United States—Juvenile literature. I. Title.

JC346.C53 2005
323.6'5'0973—dc22
                                                    2005047202

Book and cover design by Isabel Lasater Hernandez
Printed and Bound in China by Sun Fung Offset Binding Co. Ltd.

The Pledge of Allegiance

Written & Illustrated by
Barbra Clack

BRIGHT SKY PRESS   ALBANY, TEXAS

A pledge is

a promise.

"I pledge ...

... allegiance ...

... to the Flag ...

of

America

1776

... of the United States of America, ...

and
to
the

re·pub′lic (rḗ·pŭb′lĭk), *n.* A state or cou
in which those persons who have the righ
vote hold the supreme power; also, the
of government by which such a state is gove
as, the United States of America is a rep

 **Government**

for

which

it

stands

.. and to the Republic for which it stands: ...

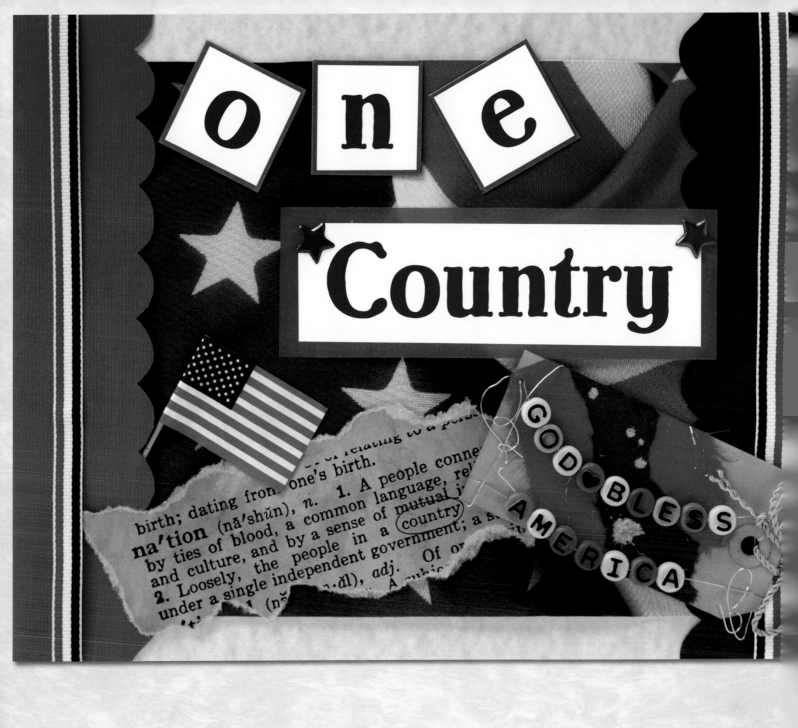

under

God

... one Nation under God, ...

... indivisible, ...

with
Freedom

... with Liberty ...

and Fairness for all

... and Justice for all."

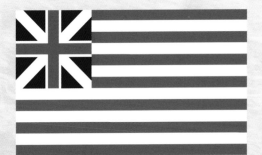

**The Grand Union or Continental Flag
1775**

An early Stars and Stripes

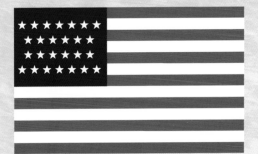

**The 26-Star Flag
1838**

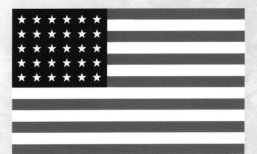

**The 30-Star Flag
1848**

**The 34-Star Flag
1861**

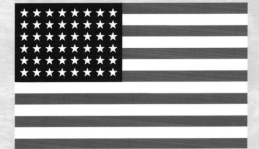

**The 48-Star Flag
1912**

The 50-Star Flag—1959

Each star on this flag is numbered to match a state's joining the Union. Can you find your state's star?

1. Delaware—1787	13. Rhode Island—1790	26. Michigan—1837	39. North Dakota—1889
2. Pennsylvania—1787	14. Vermont—1791	27. Florida—1845	40. South Dakota—1889
3. New Jersey—1787	15. Kentucky—1792	28. Texas—1845	41. Montana—1889
4. Georgia—1788	16. Tennessee—1796	29. Iowa—1846	42. Washington—1889
5. Connecticut—1788	17. Ohio—1803	30. Wisconsin—1848	43. Idaho—1890
6. Massachusetts—1788	18. Louisiana—1812	31. California—1850	44. Wyoming—1890
7. Maryland—1788	19. Indiana—1816	32. Minnesota—1858	45. Utah—1896
8. South Carolina—1788	20. Mississippi—1817	33. Oregon—1859	46. Oklahoma—1907
9. New Hampshire—1788	21. Illinois—1818	34. Kansas—1861	47. New Mexico—1912
10. Virginia—1788	22. Alabama—1819	35. West Virginia—1863	48. Arizona—1912
11. New York—1788	23. Maine—1820	36. Nevada—1864	49. Alaska—1959
12. North Carolina—1789	24. Missouri—1821	37. Nebraska—1867	50. Hawaii—1959
	25. Arkansas—1836	38. Colorado—1876	

About the Pledge

School children were the first to say the Pledge. That was in
October 1892 on the 400th anniversary of Christopher
Columbus's discovery of America! Over
12,000,000 (that's *million!*) kids said it that day.

The pledge was shorter then. It looked like this:

> I pledge allegiance to my Flag,
> and to the Republic for which it stands:
> one Nation indivisible,
> With Liberty and Justice for all.

Twenty-five years later, when these children were adults, they decided to change
the Pledge to say the **Flag of the United States** (instead of *my* Flag). One year
later, they added **of America**. After all, there is only *one Flag* of the United States

of America. These former school children did this on *Flag Day* at the first and second National Flag Conferences in Washington, D.C.

One week after Flag Day in 1942, when these school children were grandparents, the Pledge finally became part of the United States law.

In 1945 the Pledge was given its official name. (You know what it is. That's right!) Now it is called the Pledge of Allegiance.

An official name was not the last change for the Pledge of Allegiance. In 1954—again on Flag Day—the words **under God** were added to the Pledge. What began as twenty-three words has become a thirty-one word pledge *to the American way of life*—as illustrated in this book.

About the Statue of Liberty

A 100th birthday present! The Statue of Liberty was a present from France. The statue came in pieces, and a pedestal had to be built. So it took ten years after our country's 100th birthday before the Statue of Liberty was put together. *And you thought that some of your presents took a long time to put together!*

Can you find me?

Sometimes the Statue of Liberty is called "Lady Liberty." But whatever she's called, you can see her in New York Harbor, standing for friendship between countries—and for FREEDOM!

How big is she? Her mouth is 3 feet wide. Her index finger is 8 feet long. From her toes to her torch, she is 151 feet, 1 inch tall.

Can you imagine reading a book that is 2 feet thick? That's how thick Lady Liberty's tablet is.

About the Liberty Bell

The Liberty Bell is in Philadelphia, Pennsylvania, at Independence Hall.

The most important time it rang was when the Declaration of Independence was read to the citizens on July 8, 1776—only four days after the Declaration of Independence had been signed by the Continental Congress.

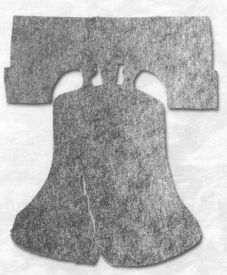

Can you find me?

When did the bell crack? No one knows when the bell *began* to crack. But the *final* crack appeared when the bell was rung on George Washington's birthday in 1846.

The name *Liberty Bell* was first used when the bell became a national symbol during the Abolitionist Movement in the mid-1880s.

About the Scales of Justice

Scales stand for fairness. They are evenly balanced and are used for weighing things. They have represented justice since the Roman times, over 2000 years ago.

Often you see a picture of a blind-folded woman holding the scales. She is called Lady Justice.

Sometime when you are sharing a piece of fruit with a friend, weigh the pieces to see if they are even!

Can you find me?

About the American Bald Eagle

The American Bald Eagle was adopted as an emblem for the United States of America in 1782. It appears on many coins and is used on the official seal of the United States of America.

The eagle was chosen because of its strength and beauty and for the freedom it enjoys as it flies.

Can you find me?

No, the eagle is not really bald.

His head is covered in white feathers, which may make him look bald from a distance.

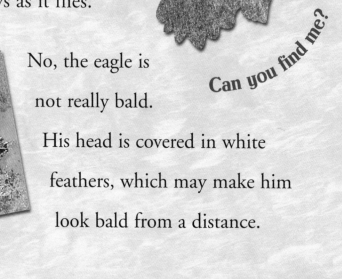

About the Flag

In the beginning, Congress was going to add a stripe and a star for each new state, but it did not take very long for people to realize that the flag would get way too big. So Congress decided just to add a star for each new state.

The thirteen stripes stand for the thirteen original states. Tradition says:

"Red symbolizes bravery.

White stands for goodness.

Blue represents fairness."

The red stripes along the top and bottom of the flag are there to help the flag show up better.

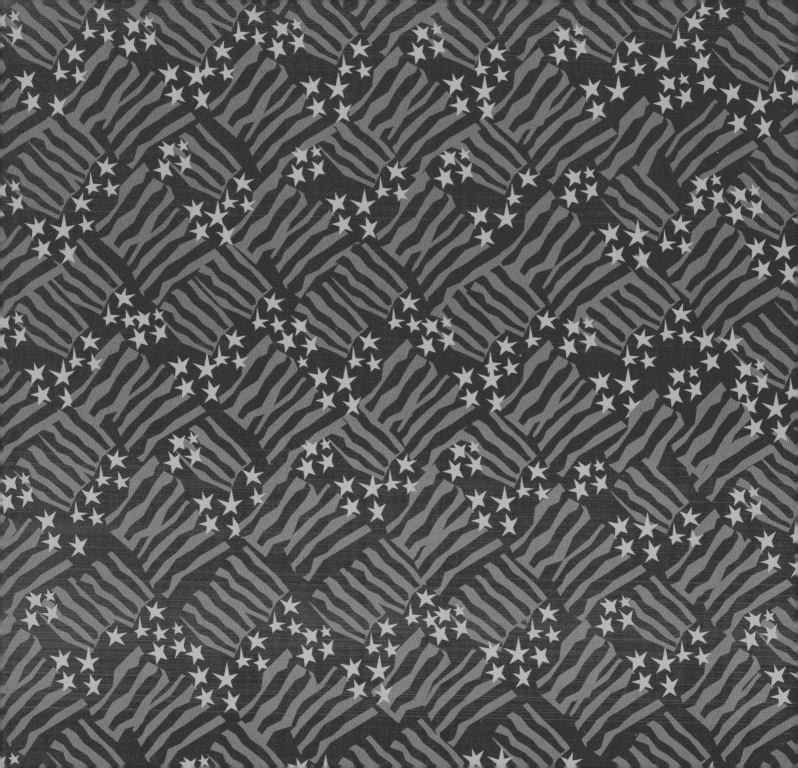